Jerry Crew arrived at his work site in the Northern California woods. As he walked toward his bulldozer, he noticed something strange in the soft dirt. Gigantic footprints!

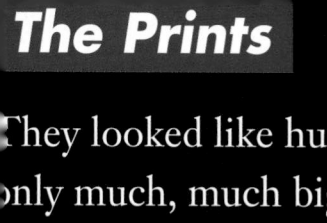

The Prints

They looked like human footprints, only much, much bigger.

As days went by, new prints continued to appear at the site. But who—or what—was making them?

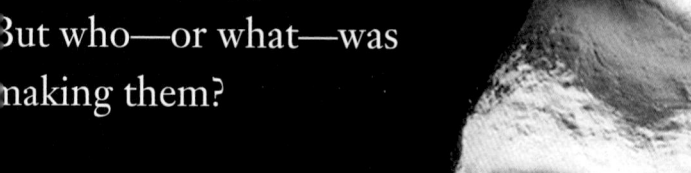

The Creature

Crew made plaster models of the prints. He showed them around. People were amazed. No creature had feet that big. *Right?*

A local newspaper gave the mysterious creature its name: Bigfoot!

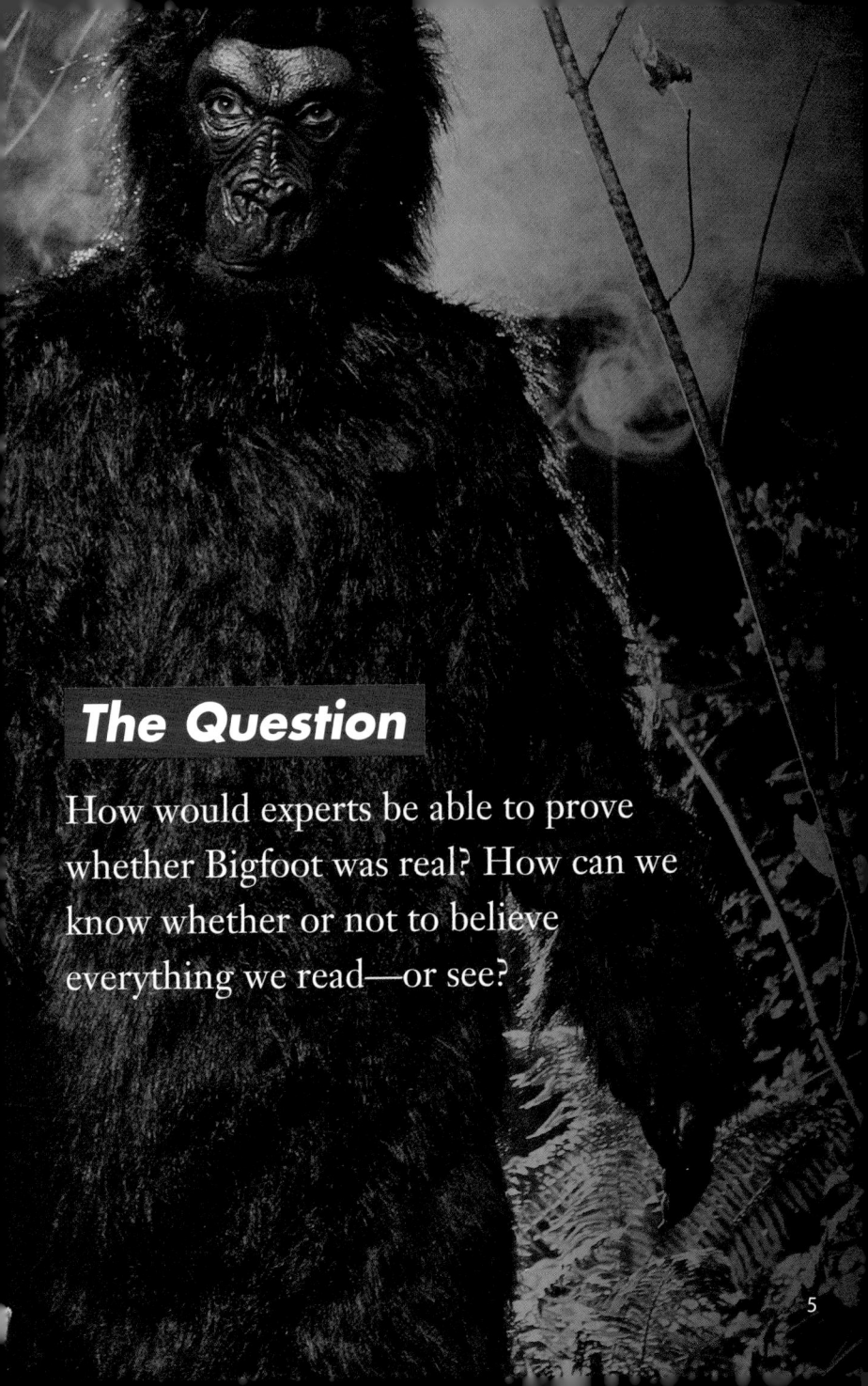

The Question

How would experts be able to prove whether Bigfoot was real? How can we know whether or not to believe everything we read—or see?

Cover design: Maria Bergós, Book&Look **Interior design:** Red Herring Design/NYC Photographs ©: cover footprints: Aurelie and Morgan David de Lossy/iStockphoto; cover forest: andreiuc88/Shutterstock; cover bigfoot: Restavr/ Dreamstime; 1: Bob Pool/Getty Images; 2-3: Anthony Robert La Penna/Bangor Daily News/The Image Works; 4-5: RyanJLane/iStockphoto; 7 footprints: Aurelie and Morgan David de Lossy/iStockphoto; 7 forest: andreiuc88/Shutterstock; 7 bigfoot: Restavr/Dreamstime; 8: Destination Truth/AFP/Newscom; 10: Bettmann/Getty Images; 12: Willow Creek China Flat Museum; 13: Friedrich Saurer/Alamy Images; 14: Popperfoto/Getty Images; 17: Alan Berner/KRT/Newscom; 18: Rue des Archives/The Granger Collection; 21: Fortean/TopFoto/The Image Works; 22-23: Adam Chiu/Red Herring; 24: Dale O'Dell/ Alamy Images; 26: AP Images; 28: Bill Schaefer/The Idaho State Journal/AP Images; 30: Suzi Eszterhas/Minden Pictures; 31: American Museum of Natural History; 32: Dave Rubert Photography; 35: Michael Nichols/National Geographic Creative; 36 top: Jackson Graham/CartoonStock; 36 bottom: Carroll Zahn/CartoonStock; 37: Randall McIlwaine/CartoonStock; 38: Jesse Harlan Alderman/AP Images; 40 binoculars: jcphoto/iStockphoto; 40 compass, map: Oleksiy Maksymenko/Alamy Images; 40 test tubes: Fedor Bobkov/Shutterstock; 40 phone: SKrow/iStockphoto; 41 water bottle: Ingram Publishing/ Alamy Images; 41 radio: Filippo Prono/Dreamstime; 41 suitcase: Norman Pogson/Shutterstock; 41 notebook: Simon C Ford/Alamy Images; 42 top: Fortean/Sibbick/TopFoto/The Image Works; 42 center: Fortean/TopFoto/The Image Works; 42 bottom: Fortean/TopFoto/The Image Works; 44 top: Topfoto/The Image Works; 44 center: Nicolle Rager/National Science Foundation; 44 bottom: Conrad Maufe/Nature Picture Library.

Library of Congress Cataloging-in-Publication Data
Names: Teitelbaum, Michael, author.
Title: Tracking Bigfoot : Is it Real or a Hoax? /
Michael Teitelbaum.
Other titles: Xbooks.
Description: [New edition] | New York, NY : Scholastic, Inc., 2020. | Series: Xbooks | Includes index. | Audience: Grades 4-6. (provided by Scholastic Inc.)
Identifiers: LCCN 2019028886| ISBN 9780531238158 (library binding) | ISBN 9780531243817 (paperback)
Subjects: LCSH: Sasquatch--Juvenile literature. | Curiosities and wonders--Juvenile literature.
Classification: LCC QL89.2.S2 T4242 2020 | DDC 001.944--dc23

Printed in the Johar Bahru, Malaysia   108

1 2 3 4 5 6 7 8 9 10 R 29 28 27 26 25 24 23 22 21 20

TRACKING BIGFOOT

Is it Real or a Hoax?

MICHAEL TEITELBAUM

TWO ADVENTURERS display a cast of what they claim is a Bigfoot footprint found in Nepal.

TABLE OF CONTENTS

THIS FOOTPRINT, **found by Phil Thompson in 1976, is almost the exact size of the prints Jerry Crew found in California decades earlier.**

1

Enormous Footprints Found!

Something strange is afoot in the forests of Northern California.

One morning in August 1958, Jerry Crew arrived at work. He was part of a team that cut logging roads through the woods of Northern California. As he walked toward his bulldozer, he noticed something strange. There were huge footprints in the newly dug road. They looked like human footprints. But they were enormous.

JERRY CREW holds a plaster cast of a footprint found at a construction site.

As days went by, new footprints continued to appear at the site. After a few weeks, Crew decided to make plaster casts, or models, of the prints. He poured wet plaster into the footprints. When it hardened, he removed the foot-shaped casts.

Really Big Feet

People were amazed. The footprints were 16 inches long and seven inches wide! No known species, or kind, of animal in the area had feet that big. The local newspaper called the beast Bigfoot.

Soon Bigfoot was the biggest cryptid in the news. (Cryptids are animals that people report seeing—but no one has proven exist.) People all over the country had heard about the cryptid with size 22 feet. The legend of Bigfoot was born.

MANY PEOPLE imagined that Bigfoot looked something like this.

THESE ENORMOUS FOOTPRINTS were photographed during a 1961 expedition to Mount Everest. They were said to have been made by a creature called a Yeti.

2

The Search Begins

Do beasts like Bigfoot live all over the world?

Native American legends tell of a Bigfoot-like beast living in the woods of the Pacific Northwest. It was said to be bigger and stronger than a bear. Some people called it *Ts'emekwes*. Others knew it as *Sæsq'ec*, or Sasquatch. Both names mean pretty much the same thing: Wild Man of the Woods.

Early European settlers in North America had described similar creatures. And many other cultures have stories of a giant ape. In the countries of Nepal and Tibet it's known as the *Yeti*, which was translated into English as the "Abominable Snowman." In Australia, it's called *Yowie*. And there are Chinese folktales about a wild man called the *Yeren*.

Searching for Bigfoot

After Jerry Crew spotted the footprints in Northern California, people began searching for Bigfoot. One of the first researchers was Roger Patterson. In 1966, he wrote a book called *Do Abominable Snowmen of America Really Exist?* The legends about such creatures, along with reported sightings, convinced him that the answer was yes.

Patterson knew that it wouldn't be enough to find footprints. To prove Bigfoot's existence, he would have to capture the cryptid on film. So he raised some money to rent a camera and make a film. Then he set out to find the hairy beast.

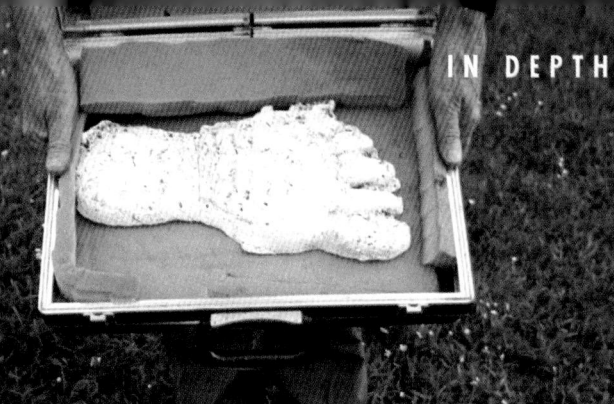

Cryptid Hunting

How do you prove the existence of something that might not be real?

Cryptozoologists have a tough job. They search for cryptids. Those are animals that some people believe are real but that have not been proven to exist.

So, what kind of evidence do cryptozoologists look for?

Images. Cryptozoologists dream of getting a photo or video of the creature they're tracking.

Footprints. If cryptid hunters come across an unusual footprint, they will collect a lot of info about it.
• They'll photograph the footprint. Before they do, they'll put something with a standard size—like a soda can—next to the print for comparison.
• They'll measure the creature's stride. That's the distance from the tip of a right footprint to the tip of the next right print.
• They'll make a plaster cast. They pour wet plaster into the print and allow it to partially harden. Then they write the date, time, and location on it.

Scat. Cryptozoologists photograph or collect any unidentifiable animal droppings—scat. They'll then compare those samples with the scat of animals that live in the area. Is this scat from a different creature?

Collect fur. They'll compare it to other animals in the area.

Sounds. If cryptozoologists get really lucky, they can record sounds that might be from a cryptid.

Eyewitnesses. There are plenty of those. But people tend to see what they want to see!

THIS IMAGE was taken from Roger Patterson's 1967 film.

3

Screen Test

Does a short film prove that Bigfoot exists?

In October 1967, Roger Patterson and his friend Bob Gimlin set out to find Bigfoot. They decided to explore an area near where Jerry Crew had found the footprints. They were riding on horseback along a mountain trail when they saw a tall, shaggy creature drinking from a stream.

The sight spooked the horses. They reared up on their hind legs. The creature noticed them and began moving away. Patterson grabbed his movie camera. He shot less than a minute of film before the creature disappeared into the woods. But Patterson had what he'd come for.

Action!

The film showed a large, apelike animal with a long stride. Researchers who went back to the site found a few big footprints. Based on the film and the footprints, they figured that the creature was close to seven feet tall and weighed from 300 to 800 pounds.

Was it Bigfoot? Or was it just a very big prank, or hoax? Many people thought it was a hoax. But Patterson said that he hadn't faked anything. And after studying the film, most Bigfoot researchers concluded that it was real. They saw the film as proof that Bigfoot existed.

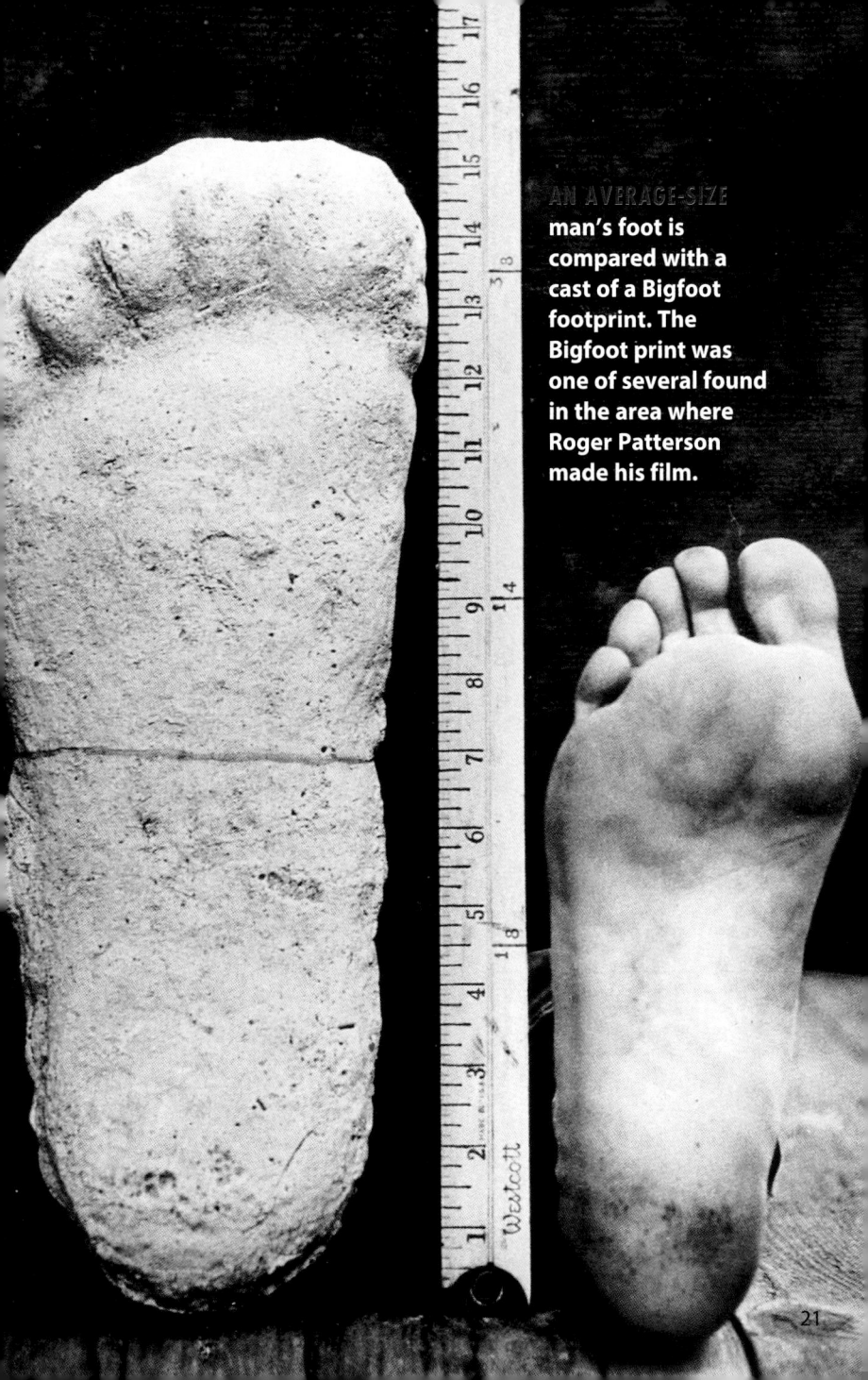

AN AVERAGE-SIZE man's foot is compared with a cast of a Bigfoot footprint. The Bigfoot print was one of several found in the area where Roger Patterson made his film.

21

Big and Tall

How would Bigfoot stack up next to some of these greats?

1 Shaquille O'Neal
HEIGHT: 7'1"
WEIGHT: 325 lbs.
FOOT LENGTH: 16.14";
shoe size: 22–23
FACT: O'Neal says:
"Because I'm so big, you have to look at me. I think of myself as a monument."
STATUS: A supersize superstar in the NBA from 1992–2011

2 Sumo wrestlers
WEIGHT: Up to 550 lbs.
FACT: To maintain their weight, these gigantic wrestlers consume about 20,000 calories a day! (An average-size man consumes about 3,000.)
STATUS: Cultural icons of Japan

3 Johann Petursson, the giant Viking
HEIGHT: 7'8"
WEIGHT: 359 lbs.
FACT: For a time, this Icelandic gentle giant was the tallest man alive. He joined an American circus and appeared in the 1981 film *Carny*.
STATUS: Died in 1984

4 Colossal squid
LENGTH: 39–46 ft.
WEIGHT: Up to 1,100 lbs.
FACT: The largest known invertebrates, these sea creatures have sharp hooks lining their limbs and the largest eyes in the animal kingdom. They live in oceans from north of Antarctica to southern South America and Africa.
STATUS: Rarely seen

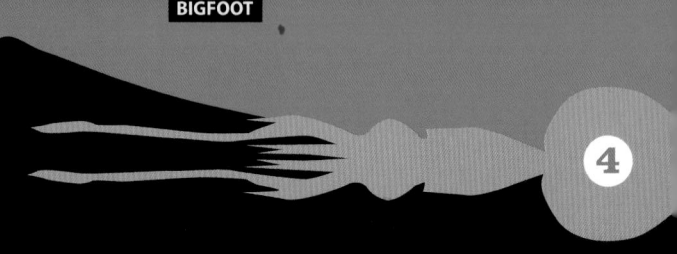

BIGFOOT

5 Woolly mammoth

HEIGHT: 9–15 ft.
WEIGHT: Up to 8 tons
FACT: This relative of the African elephant used its 17-foot-long tusks for protection, mating rituals, and digging for food in the snow.
STATUS: Extinct

6 Argentinosaurus

LENGTH: 120 ft.
WEIGHT: Over 100 tons
FACT: One vertebra of this giant dino is four feet thick!
STATUS: Extinct

7 Blue whale

LENGTH: Up to 108 ft.
WEIGHT: Up to 200 tons
FACT: For their first seven months of life, baby blues drink about 100 gallons of milk and gain about 200 pounds every day! Did we mention it's the largest animal ever?
STATUS: Endangered

8 Giant ground sloth

LENGTH: 20 ft.
WEIGHT: 2–3 tons
FACT: Standing on its hind legs, this cave dweller could reach over 20 feet high and stretch its 20-inch-long claws to grab food.
STATUS: Extinct

9 Glyptodon, the giant armadillo

LENGTH: About 10 ft.
WEIGHT: Up to 2,000 lbs.
FACT: Its shell, about the size of a VW Beetle, was used by ancient South American hunters as a shelter.
STATUS: Extinct

23

4

The Battle for Bigfoot

Is Bigfoot real?
Skeptics and believers can't agree.

It has been over 40 years since Roger Patterson made his film. In that time, thousands of Bigfoot sightings have been reported. Some people have taken photos of a creature they say is Bigfoot, but most of those photos are blurry. Other cryptid trackers have recorded sounds they claim were made by the creature. And researchers have collected lots of footprints and some fur samples. Some observers even claim they've caught a whiff of Bigfoot. They say the big guy smells nasty.

Faking Tracks

But is any of this evidence real? Probably not. Pranksters have admitted to creating a lot of it. Some claim to have strapped on big wooden feet and stomped around to make Bigfoot tracks.

One skeptic, or doubter, was a writer named Benjamin Radford. He took a close look at a lot of the evidence. He concluded that none of it was credible.

THE PERSON who took this photograph also reported hearing strange noises and smelling a strong, unusual odor.

All Bigfoot samples have been found "to be hoaxes, inconclusive, or from known animals," he writes.

Bigfoot researchers think that Radford looked at only some of the evidence. They admit that there have been many hoaxes. But they say that there is still plenty of good evidence to support their belief in Bigfoot. And a few scientists agree with them.

The Bigfoot Debate

So who is more credible—the skeptics or the believers? To decide for yourself, examine the evidence closely.

Believers: People who think Bigfoot exists say that the creature couldn't be a person in a gorilla suit, as doubters have suggested. The chest is too big. The arms are too long. It doesn't walk the way humans do.

Skeptics: The doubters find it suspicious that Patterson set out to film Bigfoot—and succeeded on his first try. They also think it's strange that no other Bigfoot has been spotted in that area since the film was made. And they point out that in 2004, a man named Bob Heironimus claimed that Patterson had hired him to wear a gorilla suit. Another man, Philip Morris, said that he made the suit.

What About the Footprints?

Believers: Cryptozoologists say that no known animal could have made the footprints. Some claim that humans wearing fake feet couldn't have made

them either. And so many prints have been found! How could pranksters be responsible for all of them?

Jeffrey Meldrum is a professor at Idaho State University. He studies the way humans and other primates walk. (Primates are the group of mammals that includes humans, monkeys, and apes.) Meldrum has collected and examined many Bigfoot footprints. In an interview with *National Geographic*, he said: "Given the scientific evidence I've examined, I'm convinced that there's a creature out there that is yet to be identified."

Skeptics: They say that the footprints are too different for one animal to have made them. They were probably made by many different pranksters.

Are Eyewitness Accounts Believable?

Believers: Bigfoot researchers agree that some reported sightings are hoaxes. But they say that the thousands of people who claim to have seen a Bigfoot can't all be lying, mistaken, or crazy.

Skeptics: Eyewitness accounts aren't always reliable. For example, somebody in an area considered "Bigfoot country" might see a bear in the distance and decide it's a Bigfoot. It's called wishful thinking. You see what you want to see.

One More Thing ...

Believers: They point out that people once thought that the African mountain gorilla was a myth. Then one was killed in 1902, and the myth became reality. And for decades sailors told tales of an enormous squid that was bigger than a whale. People thought those stories were full of water—until researchers finally captured one on film!

Skeptics: They say that the biggest reason to doubt Bigfoot's existence is that no body or skeleton has ever been found.

THE MOUNTAIN GORILLA of central Africa does exist. But it is so rarely seen that people once thought it was a myth.

Human, Beast, or Both?

What exactly is Bigfoot?

Cryptozoologists think that Bigfoot must be a new species of ape. One of the first and most respected Bigfoot researchers was Dr. Grover Krantz. His theory was that Bigfoot was the living relative of an extinct ape called *Gigantopithecus blacki.*

Cryptozoologists estimate that there are a few thousand Bigfoots alive today. They describe the creature as shy. They also say that it's nocturnal—comes out only at night. Maybe that's why it's so hard to find!

A MODEL OF
Gigantopithecus blacki

RAY WALLACE'S nephew Dale poses with his uncle's fake Bigfoot feet.

5

Shocking Confession!

A prankster is exposed.
Or is it just another hoax?

In 2002, the press reported a shocking story. The family of a man named Ray Wallace was claiming that Wallace had made the huge footprints that Jerry Crew found in 1958.

Wallace was Jerry Crew's boss. He was known as a practical joker. And Wallace bragged that he had used wooden "track stompers" to make the famous footprints.

Bigfoot, or Big Joke?

When Wallace died in 2002, the family told his story. It made headlines around the country. Crew's discovery of the footprints had started the Bigfoot craze. Many people saw Wallace's story as proof that Bigfoot doesn't exist.

But Bigfoot researchers laughed. They said that Wallace's claim that he was "the father of Bigfoot" was just a final hoax. And they said that his stompers didn't even match the tracks that Crew found.

What's your opinion? Do you think that an undiscovered ape species exists? Do you think it's likely that such a creature made the footprints that Crew found in California? How about Roger Patterson's movie? Did he really capture Bigfoot on film?

Primate Expert

One respected scientist surprised everyone with her opinion. Jane Goodall is highly regarded for her work with chimpanzees. In 2003, she told an interviewer that she was sure that Bigfoot exists. But by the end of the interview, Goodall sounded less certain. "Maybe they don't exist, but I want them to," she said.

Her spokesperson later clarified Goodall's position: "As a scientist, she's very curious and she keeps an open mind," the spokesperson said. "She's fascinated by [the question]."

So are many other people. But unless somebody catches a Bigfoot, or a body or skeleton is found, most scientists will remain skeptical. **X**

JANE GOODALL **with some of the chimps she studies in Tanzania, Africa**

Joke's on Bigfoot

Real or not, Bigfoot is good for a giggle.

You'll probably never spot Bigfoot in the wild. But there's no way you'll miss seeing this creature in popular culture. There's a monster truck called Bigfoot, a Bigfoot action figure, and even movies about the beast! The big hairy guy also appears in cartoons. Here's a look at a few of them.

" IT LOOKS TO ME AS THOUGH THE YETI'S INTO LINE DANCING "

"I GIVE UP.. WHAT IS NINE FEET TALL AND HAS TWO FANGS AND HAS HAIR ALL OVER ITS BODY ?"

Bigfoot Hunter

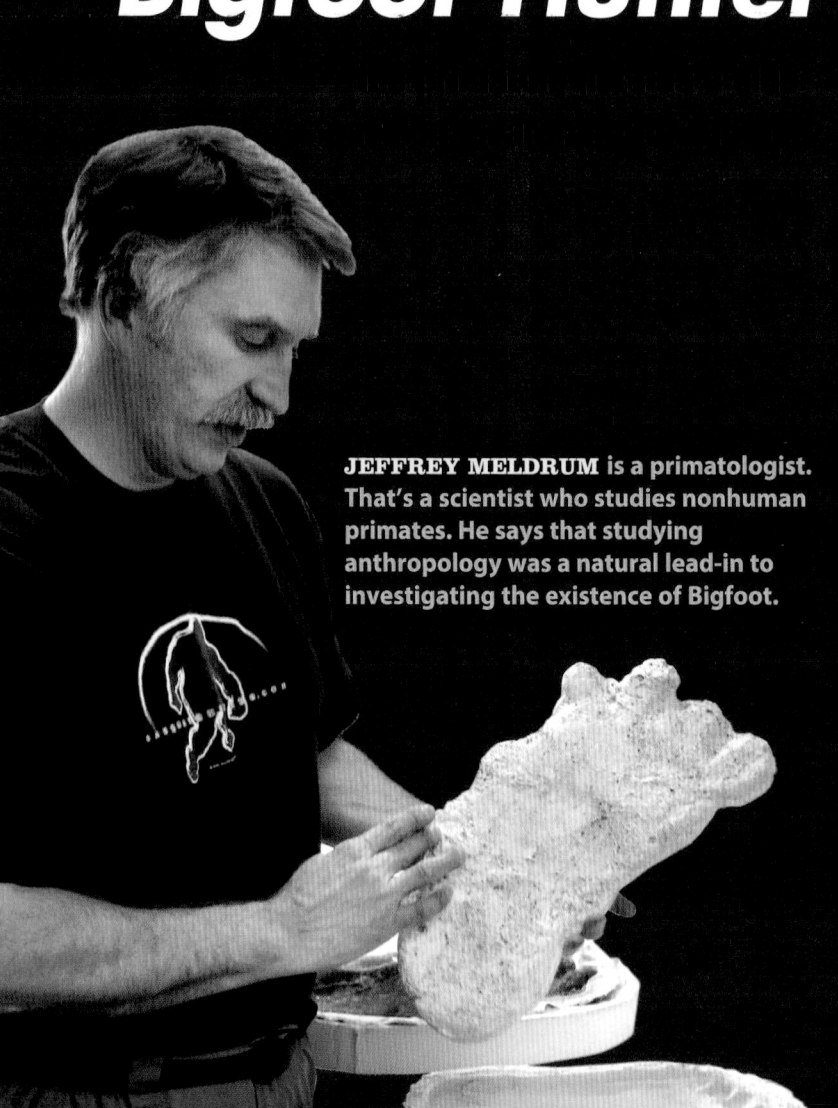

JEFFREY MELDRUM is a primatologist. That's a scientist who studies nonhuman primates. He says that studying anthropology was a natural lead-in to investigating the existence of Bigfoot.

What can footprints tell you about a creature?
DR. JEFFREY MELDRUM: As a primatologist, I study how the foot bends and moves when a two-legged animal walks. The way an ape walks is different from the way a human walks.

Say you have a plaster cast of an extremely large footprint. How does it help your research on Bigfoot?
MELDRUM: You learn that it was made by an animal that doesn't walk like a human. That provides strong evidence that the track was made by Sasquatch. [Bigfoot researchers often use the word "Sasquatch" rather than "Bigfoot."]

What was your first experience with Sasquatch?
MELDRUM: In 1996 I went to visit [a cryptozoologist named] Paul Freeman and saw his collection of casts. Then he showed me some fresh tracks. I made some plaster casts of these tracks and began my own collection and study.

Describe what you do when you find some tracks.
MELDRUM: I rule out any chance of a hoax. Then I make a cast. I also try to interview any local witnesses who claim to have seen the animal that made the tracks.

What's your favorite thing about your job?
MELDRUM: Working on the forefront of what could be the discovery of a previously unknown species on Earth.

What advice do you have for young people interested in this subject?
MELDRUM: Study as much about anthropology and animal biology as you can. You need a solid basic knowledge about animals we do know exist (like apes) if you are trying to discover the existence of new species. Also, don't let the skeptics discourage you from your investigations. But always be careful of hoaxes.

Poop Patrol

When primatologists go into the field, they don't let anything go to waste.

1 Specimen tubes
Primatologists are very interested in excrement—poop. They use specimen tubes to collect stinky samples in the field. The samples will help them learn about primates' diets.

2 Binoculars
A pair of binoculars helps primatologists observe dangerous primates from a safe distance.

3 Compass, map, and GPS
These navigational tools can help primatologists find their way through dense jungles and unfamiliar territory.

4 Small suitcase
Primatologists travel light on expeditions. The smaller the suitcase, the easier it is to carry through wild areas.

5 Water bottle and filters

A water bottle with a built-in filter helps protect researchers from drinking dirty water when they're in the field.

6 Radio transmitter

It's important for primatologists to have a way to communicate with base camp in case a problem comes up. Some primatologists might also use a cell phone for this purpose.

7 Field log

As they observe primates in the wild, primatologists take notes in a field log. Later, they use these notes to write up field reports describing what they saw. Some primatologists also use digital devices to take notes and shoot video.

Meet the Cryptids!

	First Sighting
Chupacabra (or "Goatsucker")	Puerto Rico in the early 1990s
Ogopogo	Okanagan Lake, Canada. Native American legends tell of a great serpent that lived in the lake. People offered it sacrifices so they could cross the lake safely.
Florida Skunk Ape	Occasional sightings have been reported in the southeastern United States for 200 years. There have been about 75 sightings in the past 20 years.

Evidence For	Evidence Against
Locals reported sightings of a strange creature, as well as the mysterious deaths of farm animals. Some people believed that a creature was killing the animals and sucking their blood.	Tests in Puerto Rico by the National Geographic Channel showed that the dead animals had been killed by other animals or by people.
There have been many eyewitness reports. Whole groups of people have claimed to see Ogopogo at the same time.	The monster in legends was fierce and evil. Modern eyewitnesses describe the one they've seen as playful. The typical behaviors of real animals don't change over time.
The best evidence is two photos taken by an elderly Florida couple in 2000. They said that they saw (and smelled!) an apelike animal in their backyard. Cryptozoologists think it might have been a skunk ape, a cryptid known for its terrible odor.	Many of the reported sightings were in the Big Cypress Swamp in Florida. It's strange that the park rangers who work there have never seen one. Most rangers think the skunk ape is probably a hoax.

Mokèlé-Mbèmbé

For more than 200 years, people in central Africa have been telling visitors about a swamp-dwelling, dinosaur-like creature called Mokèlé-Mbèmbé.

Loch Ness Monster

There have been many legends about a whalelike creature that lived in the waters of Scotland's Loch Ness.

Giant Squid

In 1853, some Danish fishermen found the remains of what seemed to have been giant squid.

Several teams have searched for this living dinosaur. Local people told stories about seeing the creature. Some reported finding large footprints. A few team explorers claimed they'd seen or heard the creature.

There are no clear photos or videos of this cryptid.

Many people claimed to have seen this beast. In 1934, Robert Wilson snapped a photo of what he said was the monster.

Over the years, there have been many scientific studies of the lake, one lasting ten years. In 2003, scientist Ian Florence concluded, "There is nothing there."

In 2004, a scientist named Tsunemi Kubodera photographed hundreds of giant squid. He used a camera attached to a line that went to a depth of 2,950 feet. Sunlight can't reach that depth, so the camera had lights attached to it. The photos prove that these enormous creatures really exist!

None. The giant squid is no longer a cryptid. Scientists accept that it's a real animal.

RESOURCES

Here's a selection of books for more information about cryptids and other mysterious creatures.

What to Read Next

NONFICTION

Halls, Kelly Milner. *In Search of Sasquatch*. New York: HMH Books for Young Readers, 2011.

Hoaxed!: Fakes and Mistakes in the World of Science (by the Editors of YES Mag). Tonawanda, New York: Kids Can Press, 2009.

Johnson, C. M. *Creatures* (Origins: Urban Legends). Minneapolis, Minnesota: Full Tilt Press, 2017.

Karst, Ken. *Loch Ness Monster* (Enduring Mysteries). Mankato, Minnesota: The Creative Company, 2014.

Peabody, Erin. *The Loch Ness Monster* (Behind the Legend). New York: Little Bee Books, 2017.

Teitelbaum, Michael. *Bigfoot Caught on Film: And Other Monster Sightings!* (24/7: Science Behind the Scenes, Mystery Files). New York: Scholastic Library Publishing, 2008.

Wright, John D. *Cryptids and Other Creepy Creatures: The World of Unsolved Mysteries*. New York: Scholastic, 2009.

FICTION

Eagar, Lindsay. *The Bigfoot Files*. Somerville, Massachusetts: Candlewick Press, 2018.

Fisher, Lija. *The Cryptid Catcher* (The Cryptid Duology). New York: Farrar, Straus and Giroux, 2018.

Flitcroft, Jean. *The Loch Ness Monster* (The Cryptid Files). Minneapolis, Minnesota: Darby Creek, 2010.

Savage, Melissa. *Lemons*. New York: Crown Books for Young Readers, 2017.

Sherry, Kevin. *Meet the Bigfeet* (The Yeti Files #1). New York: Scholastic Press, 2014.

Smith, Roland. *Chupacabra*. New York: Scholastic Press, 2013.

Smith, Roland. *Cryptid Hunters*. New York: Hyperion Books for Children, 2006.

anthropology (AN-thruh-POL-uh-jee) *noun* the study of the customs and social structures of humans, including human myths and legends

biology (bye-OL-uh-jee) *noun* the scientific study of living things

conclude (kuhn-KLOOD) *verb* to arrive at a decision based on the facts

credible (KRED-uh-buhl) *adjective* believable

cryptid (KRIP-tid) *noun* an animal that some people believe is real but whose existence has not been scientifically proven

cryptozoologist (KRIP-toh-zoh-OL-uh-jist) *noun* a researcher who studies cryptids

culture (KUHL-chur) *noun* a set of ideas, customs, and traditions shared among a group of people

endangered (en-DAYN-jurd) *adjective* at risk of becoming extinct

evidence (EV-uh-duhnss) *noun* information or objects used to prove something or to argue that something is true

expedition (ek-spuh-DISH-uhn) *noun* a journey for a special purpose, such as exploring

extinct (ek-STINGKT) *adjective* completely wiped out as a species

GPS (GEE PEE ESS) *noun* short for "Global Positioning System," a device that uses satellites to pinpoint the exact location of the user on Earth

hoax (HOHKS) *noun* an act or trick designed to fool people into believing something is true

inconclusive (in-kuhn-KLOO-siv) *adjective* not clear or not certain

invertebrate (in-VUR-tuh-brit) *noun* an animal without a backbone

legend (LEJ-uhnd) *noun* a story that has been passed down from earlier times and that has not been proven to be true

species (SPEE-sheez) *noun* a group of organisms that share specific characteristics and can mate to produce offspring

INDEX

Metric Conversions

Feet to meters: 1 ft is about 0.3 m
Miles to kilometers: 1 mi is about 1.6 km
Pounds to kilograms: 1 lb is about 0.45 kg
Ounces to grams: 1 oz is about 28 g